Chaplin

Chaplin

Nick Yapp

endeavour

Chaplin is part of the series of books on Hollywood and Rock Icons.
The design was initiated by Paul Welti, but created by Ros Holder.
Author Nick Yapp worked closely with picture researcher Jennifer
Jeffrey. The book was edited by Mark Fletcher and proofread by
Liz Ihre. Mary Osborne led the production.

Endeavour London Ltd
21-31 Woodfield Road
London W9 2BA

ISBN 978-1-873913-34-5

Printed and bound in China

Frontispiece: The Tramp with the World
at his feet… Young Chaplin sails home at
the pinnacle of his career.
Title page: Stars of Screen and Court:
(*left to right*) William T. "Big Bill" Tilden (US
Open Tennis Champion), Chaplin, Douglas
Fairbanks Senior, and the Spanish tennis star,
Manuel Alonso. Chaplin and Fairbanks were
both tennis fans; Chaplin had a court at his
studios, Fairbanks had one at his Hollywood
Mansion, "Pickfair".
Right: After making *City Lights,* Chaplin
enjoys a skiing holiday in the United States.

Contents

CHAPTER 1

A Soldier in Fred Karno's Army

(1889-1914)

Schoolboy

Charles Spencer Chaplin was born on April 16, 1889 – the second of two boys born to Charles Chaplin senior and Lily Harley. Chaplin's father was a singer-songwriter of some repute in the music halls of late Victorian London. His mother was also a professional singer, but in private was a devastatingly good mimic and comedienne, and it was her influence that decided Chaplin's career.

When Chaplin senior abandoned his wife and children, Lily had a breakdown. She was taken to the Cane Hill asylum, and the children were taken into care. Older brother Sydney was sent to the *Exmouth*, a training ship for poor boys destined for a life in the Royal Navy; seven-year-old Charlie went to the Central London Poor Law School at Hanwell, an institution of average brutality.

All his life, Chaplin was a great survivor. His mother recovered and set up home with Chaplin in Kennington, London. Chaplin ran errands, found things to sell, ate from garbage bins, and picked up the tricks of the street entertainer. He seldom attended school, which resulted in literacy problems that embarrassed him for much of his life.

Chaplin's first professional appearance of any importance was with the Eight Lancashire Lads at the Theatre Royal, Manchester on Christmas Day 1898. The Lads performed a series of spirited clog dances and Chaplin mastered the art from scratch in six weeks. Once that was done, Chaplin added his own improvised comedy business to the Lads' routines. The other seven Lancashire Lads might not have appreciated this wayward innovation; the audience loved it. One year later Chaplin left the Lads.

Enter the Clown

The next few years were hard for Chaplin. His father died of alcoholism, and his mother had to return to the Cane Hill asylum. Chaplin himself was frequently homeless, hungry, and ill. He also lost the support and protection of his older brother Sydney, who was at sea, working as a steward on the South African Line. Professionally, Chaplin had little success, partly because he was stubborn and not inclined to accept the restrictions of the material he was asked to perform. He was not sufficiently well known to be allowed a solo spot, and he took unkindly to direction – to shaping his act to fit in with those of his co-performers.

Life improved greatly in 1906 with the return of Sydney, who helped him gain employment with a teenage theatrical group known as Casey's Court Circus, a vaudeville act specializing in parodies of the acts of music hall stars. Chaplin's major roles here were in a burlesque of the story of Dick Turpin, and as "Doctor" Walford Brodie, "The Electrical Wizard of the North". Chaplin mimicked Brodie's own music hall act as magician, hypnotist, clairvoyant, and ventriloquist to perfection.

In the same year, Chaplin made a grotesque attempt to launch himself as a solo act at Foresters Music Hall in Bethnal Green, a small theater in the center of the Jewish quarter. In Chaplin's words: "My comedy was mostly anti-Semitic, and my jokes were not only old ones, but very poor, like my Jewish accent… The audience started throwing coins and orange peel, and stamping their feet and booing… When I came off the stage, I went straight to the dressing-room, took off my make-up, left the theater and never returned."

The Legitimate Stage

At the beginning of his career, Chaplin's ambition was to be an actor. In between working as a sales assistant (at a branch of W H Smith), a pageboy, a glassblower, and a printer. Chaplin toured the theatrical agencies in the West End of London, seeking work on the stage. He was persistent, and eventually received a postcard inviting him to call at Blackmore's Agency, just off the Strand.

Chaplin lied about his age, adding a couple of years, and was offered the part of the pageboy Billy in a West End production of *Sherlock Holmes*. The salary was two pounds ten shillings a week (£2.50), an enormous sum to Chaplin, who nevertheless took his time accepting the role, saying "I must consult my brother about the terms". Sydney, later Chaplin's manager for many years, did what he could to increase the offer, but without success.

There remained the problem that Chaplin could barely read, but he learned his lines by having Sydney repeatedly read them to him.

AND WILLIAM GILLETTE
ENTITLED

SHERLOCK HOLMES

BEING A HITHERTO UNPUBLISHED EPISODE
IN THE CAREER OF THE GREAT DETECTIVE
AND SHOWING HIS CONNECTION WITH THE

STRANGE CASE OF MISS FAULKNER

CHARACTERS IN THE PLAY	COMPANY APPEARING IN THE CAST
SHERLOCK HOLMES	WILLIAM GILLETTE
DOCTOR WATSON	KENNETH RIVINGTON
JOHN FORMAN	EUGENE MAYEUR
SIR EDWARD LEIGHTON	REGINALD DANCE
COUNT VON STAHLBURG	FREDERICK MORRIS
PROFESSOR MORIARTY	GEORGE SUMNER
JAMES LARRABEE	FRANCIS CARLYLE
SIDNEY PRINCE	QUINTON McPHERSON
ALFRED BASSICK	WILLIAM H. DAY
JIM CRAIGIN	CHRIS WALKER
THOMAS LEARY	HENRY WALTERS
"LIGHTFOOT" McTAGUE	WALTER DISON
JOHN	THOMAS QUINTON
PARSONS	G. MERTON
BILLY	CHARLES CHAPLIN
ALICE FAULKNER	MARIE DORO
MRS. FAULKNER	DE OLIA WEBSTER
MADGE LARRABEE	ADELAIDE PRINCE
THERESE	SYBIL CAMPBELL
MRS. SMEEDLEY	ETHEL LORRIMORE

THE PLACE IS LONDON
THE TIME TEN YEARS AGO

FIRST ACT—DRAWING ROOM AT THE LARRABEES'—EVENING
SECOND ACT—Scene I—PROFESSOR MORIARTY'S
UNDERGROUND OFFICE—MORNING
Scene II—SHERLOCK HOLMES' APARTMENTS
IN BAKER STREET—EVENING
THIRD ACT—THE STEPNEY GAS CHAMBER—MIDNIGHT
FOURTH ACT—DOCTOR WATSON'S CONSULTING ROOM KENSINGTON—THE
FOLLOWING EVENING

SCENERY BY ERNEST GROS   INCIDENTAL MUSIC BY WILLIAM FURST

INTERMISSIONS

Between the 1st and 2nd Acts, 9 minutes
Between the 2nd and 3rd Acts, 7 minutes
Between the 3rd and 4th Acts, 5 minutes

MATINEE every Saturday at 2.15 o'clock

BUSINESS MANAGER—JAMES W MATHEWS   ACTING MANAGER—ROBERT M EBERLE
STAGE MANAGER—WILLIAM POSTANCE   MUSICAL DIRECTOR—JOHN CROOK

ICED TEA AND COFFEE can be had of the Attendants.

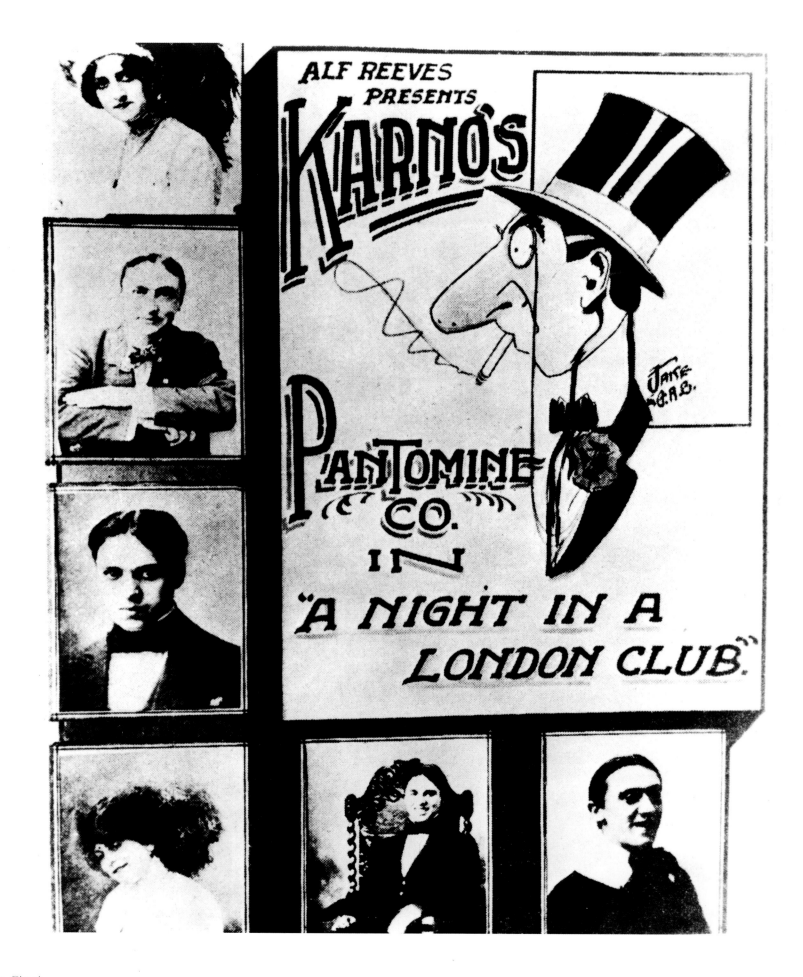

A Soldier in Fred Karno's Army

After the nightmare of being booed off the stage at Foresters Music Hall, Chaplin encountered what seemed to him a long series of theatrical disasters. What disturbed him was the discovery that he was not by nature a vaudeville comedian: "I had not that intimate, come-hither faculty with an audience". He tried being a character comedian, but that too failed. At the age of seventeen, he found himself playing the juvenile lead in a sketch, opposite a gin-sodden elderly actress. He tried writing sketches, but had difficulty selling them.

Chaplin's luck changed when brother Sydney obtained work for both of them with Fred Karno's Speechless Comedians. Karno was known as "The Guv'nor". He was a man of immense prestige in the business, and his company (Fred's Fun Business) employed over 200 artists in thirty touring companies spread around the world. Chaplin began on a two-week trial at the Shepherd's Bush Empire in a slapstick sketch called *The Football Match*.

The lead comedian was Harry Weldon, who played the goalkeeper. Chaplin noticed that there was not a single laugh in the sketch until Weldon's entrance, and resolved to change this: "I entered with my back to the audience – an idea of my own. From the back I looked immaculate, dressed in a frock-coat, top hat, cane and spats… Then I turned, showing my red nose. There was a laugh…" Chaplin went on to create "business" with a dumb-bell, his own cane, a punch-bag, and his own trousers.

Weldon was not best pleased, but after a single performance, Karno offered Chaplin a two-year contract. The next stop was to be the United States.

Left: A publicity shot of a clean-handed Fred Karno preparing one of his Boats for Hire at *Karsino*, his hotel, concert pavilion, and leisure complex on Tagg's Island in the Thames.
Above: *Karsino*. When the hotel opened on May 18, 1913, guests included Lord Birkenhead, F. E. Smith, Lord Curzon, and C. B. Cochran. The venture proved expensive to run, especially in bad weather, and three bad summers in the early 1920s forced Karno into bankruptcy.

America

In 1910, Chaplin, Karno, Stan Jefferson (better known as Stan Laurel), and a dozen other members of the Guv'nor's troupe sailed for the United States. Chaplin's inclusion in the group was largely thanks to Alf Reeves, one of Karno's recruiting officers, who was later to serve as General Manager of the Chaplin Studios for twenty-eight years. They sailed on the *SS Cairnrona*, described by Laurel as "more a cattle boat than a liner", and when New York City was sighted, Chaplin ran to the side of the ship and shouted, "America, I am coming to conquer you!" He saw the United States as a new beginning, a land in which he could put past misery and failure out of his mind, because in "the States the prospects were brighter".

Keystone

In 1913, Chaplin signed with the New York Motion Picture Company to work at their Keystone Studios in Los Angeles for $150 a week. He left for Hollywood and the world of the silent movie. He was now completely on his own and, in movie terms, an absolute novice. When he arrived at the gates to the Keystone Studios, his nerve failed him. He hung around, sick with anxiety, and almost paralyzed with fear. It took him three days to muster the courage to pass through the gates and seek out the office of Michael Sinnott, better known as Mack Sennett "The King of Comedy", and recognized at Keystone as "The Chief".

Chaplin's relationship with Mack Sennett did not get off to an auspicious start. There was little or no room in Sennett's slapstick films for character development, pathos or what Karno called "wistfulness". Keystone comedies were invented on the spot, with one gag leading to another, until the film ended in the obligatory mayhem of yet another chase.

Left: Chaplin (*on left*) with Alf Reeves (*second from right*), and two other members of the Karno company, 1911. Reeves acted as manager for the Karno troupe in the USA, and Chaplin suggested that he and Reeves form a partnership to buy the rights to make films of all of Karno's sketches.

First Films

Chaplin's first Keystone film was *Making a Living*, directed by Henry Lehrman, an unfriendly man of considerable conceit. Chaplin played the part of an "elegant swell", a role he had often performed in music halls; Lehrman played Chaplin's rival for the love of the heroine. It was a recipe for trouble. During the three days it took to make the film, Chaplin and Lehrman grew to dislike each other intensely. Years later Chaplin wrote: "When I saw the finished film, it broke my heart, for the cutter had butchered it beyond recognition, cutting into the middle of all my funny business." It's a revealing statement, a clear indication that from the start, Chaplin looked for artistry as well as comedy in his films. The Sennett system was too blunt an instrument for him.

Chaplin's instinct was to quit. He told Chester Conklin, another Keystone star, that he couldn't stand the confusion, the fact that he couldn't actually tell what he was doing. Conklin told him to stick with it. It was sound advice. Less than a week later came a pivotal moment in the history of the cinema.

It was a rainy February afternoon. Shooting was impossible. Sennett and his leading comedians were playing cards, Chaplin was aimlessly wandering about. According to legend and to Chaplin himself, Chaplin began rummaging through the costumes in the men's dressing room. He selected a pair of Fatty Arbuckle's baggy trousers, Sterling Ford's huge shoes, Conklin's tight-fitting coat, a derby hat, a snippet of crêpe hair, and a highly flexible cane. Then he gazed at himself in the dressing-room mirror and discovered that he had created the Little Tramp.

Left: Chaplin dancing with Marie Dressler in *Tillie's Punctured Romance*, made in December 1914. The film was directed by Mack Sennett and took forty-five days to make, considerably longer than any other film Chaplin made with Keystone.
Right: (*left to right*) Edgar Kennedy, Chaplin, and Mabel Normand in *Getting Acquainted*, released in December 1914. Kennedy was known as "The Master of the Slow Burn", and this was the last film he made with Chaplin.

A Change of Direction

Sennett backed the idea of Chaplin presenting his new character on screen, and the Little Tramp made film debut in *Kid Auto Races in Venice*. Henry Lehrman was again the director, and the entire film was shot in forty-five minutes. Sennett was astute enough to see that the Chaplin-Lehrman partnership was going nowhere. He handed Chaplin over to Mabel Normand — comedienne, director, and Sennett's former lover. Though Chaplin disliked working for a woman director at first, within a month the Little Tramp was a hit, and orders for Keystone films from nickelodeon companies more than doubled.

Above: The Tramp's first appearance on film. Chaplin in *Kid Auto Races at Venice*, with the infamous director Henry Lehrman (*right*) and cameraman Frank D. Williams (*left*)

Above Chaplin faces up to his rival "Masher" (Ford Sterling) in Chaplin's fourth film for Keystone, *Between Showers*. The couple in the background are Chester Conklin and Emma Clifton. It was the first of Chaplin's archetypal "a park, a policeman, and a pretty girl" pictures.

Above and opposite: Two sheets of Chaplin color transfers issued in the mid-1910s. Such was his meteoric rise to fame that Chaplin ephemera appeared very early in his career.

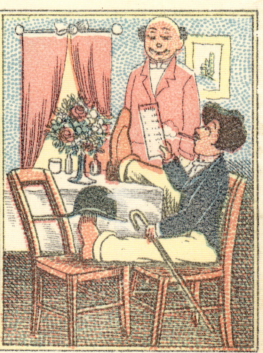

DIRECTIONS. For Successful Transfer of Pictures, Follow Instructions. Immerge the Picture in water once, quickly remove and place on the space where it is desired. Press down gently but firmly: wet the back a trifle more and after a few seconds, place the first three fingers on the Transfer and slowly draw downward until the sheet is entirely removed. Never attempt lifting the corners,-this will spoil the Picture.

Above: Chaplin as the Waiter in
Caught in a Cabaret, made in April
1914. Mabel Normand (*seated at
table*) was the female lead. In all, they
made twelve films together.

Above: Chaplin with Fritz Schade (as the Bakery Proprietor) in *Dough and Dynamite*, made in October 1914. The film took nine days to make, at a cost of $1,800. As this was $800 over budget, Chaplin lost his $25-a-film bonus. The film, however, was a tremendous success.

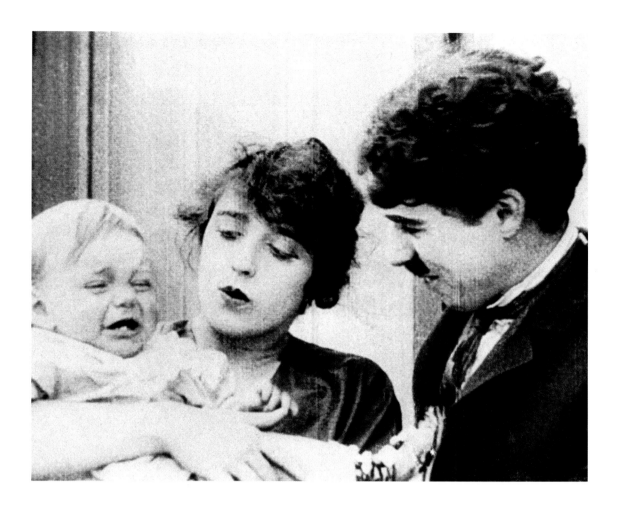

Farewell to Keystone

It didn't take long for Chaplin to persuade Sennett to let him direct his own films. It was enough for Sennett that the profits rolled in and the Little Tramp was a huge international success. Chaplin displayed a natural talent for making silent movie comedies. He didn't need words or an elaborate set. "All I need," Chaplin told Sennett, "is a park, a policeman, and a pretty girl."

He also told Sennett that he wanted a rise, and demanded $1,000 a week. Sennett was appalled; it was more than he made. Chaplin insisted. Sennett refused to give in. There was less than a

month before Chaplin's contract with Keystone expired. An offer came from Carl Laemmle of the Universal Company – twelve cents a foot (between $250 and $300 a film). It was not enough.

Chaplin still held out. At the last minute, Jess Robbins of the Essanay Company offered Chaplin $1,250 a week, plus a signing-on bonus of $10,000. Chaplin accepted. He finished cutting his last film for Sennett one Saturday night, made no farewells, and started at Essanay the following Monday. The bonus never arrived.

Opposite: Chaplin (as Weakchin) and Mack Swain (as Ling Lowbrow) in *His Prehistoric Past,* made in December 1914. It was Chaplin's last film for Keystone, and he later wrote of it: "It was a strain because it was hard to concentrate with so many business propositions dangling before me."

Above: Chaplin as the Husband, with Mabel Normand as the Wife, in *His Trysting Place.* The film was made in November 1914, and was his thirty-second for Keystone. By then Chaplin had taken almost full control of all of his films – as star, editor, writer, and director. At the time, he described Normand as "Sweet Mabel – twenty, pretty and charming, everybody's favorite."

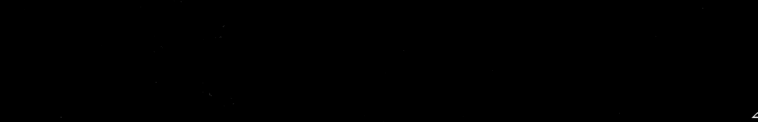

CHAPTER 2
The Tramp Joins the Artists
(1915-1930)

The Filmmaker

By the time he left Sennett in December 1914, Chaplin was an accomplished filmmaker. He knew how to shoot, direct, and edit film, and in the next five years he honed and developed these skills to such effect that in 1919, at the age of thirty, he was able to build his own film studios. The achievement was astounding. It helped that Chaplin was in the right place at the right time, but his meteoric rise in the movie business was mainly due to restless ambition, an innate business sense (shared by his manager, brother Sydney), and his own comedy genius.

Chaplin was not an easy man to work with. He was vain, short-tempered perfectionist, and a control freak. He decided where the camera should be placed, how a scene should be lit, how a set should be dressed, and exactly how his players should perform. Before the cameras rolled, Chaplin would act the part of policeman, drunk, pretty girl, or harassed husband, and actors simply re-produced what he had shown them.

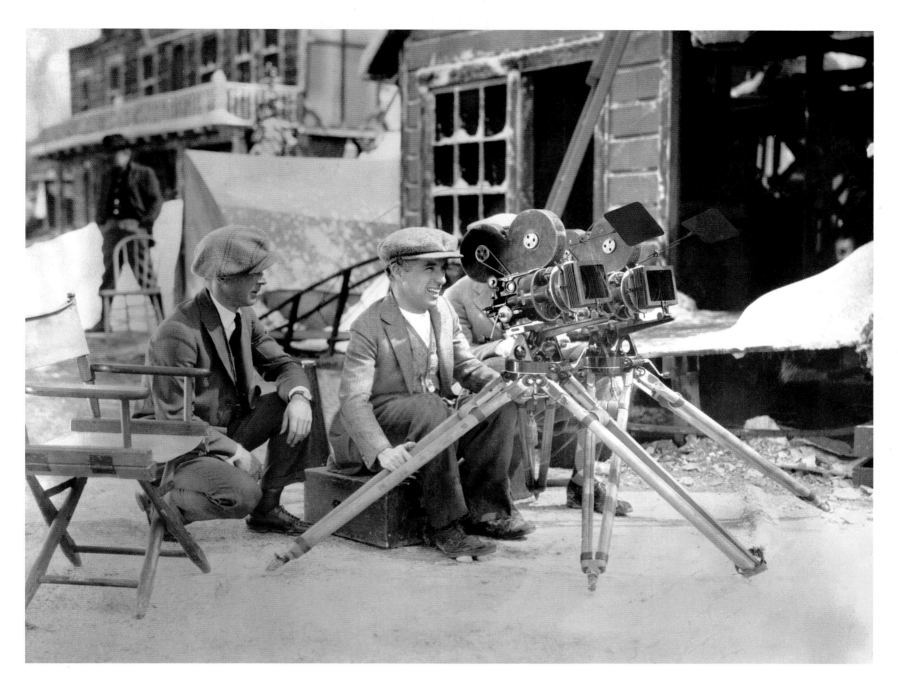

Previous page: Chaplin at the gates of his own studios, 1919.
Opposite: The young studio boss behind one of his cameras.
Above: Chaplin with two of his photographers, Roland Totheroh and Jack Wilson, on the set of *The Gold Rush*, 1925.

The Comedy Star

Chaplin spent just over a year at the Essanay Studios, from January 1915 to April 1916. His most famous film from this time was a two-reeler called *The Tramp*. In essence, the storyline was that of most Chaplin's films. The Tramp falls foul of three country hobos, one of whom is engaged to be married to the farmer's beautiful daughter. The hobos attempt to rob the farm; the Tramp drives them off. What makes the film remarkable is its wistfully unhappy ending, for the Tramp sees that, not only can he never be worthy of the woman he loves, but also she already loves another. The film ends with the Tramp shuffling away from the camera down a dirt road. Audiences gasped and sobbed, but Chaplin knew from his music hall days that tears can be every bit as addictive as laughter, and they would be back for more.

Left: Chaplin stripped for action in *The Champion*, released by Essanay in March 1915. Like many silent movie comedians, Chaplin was an accomplished acrobat with a muscular body. There were times, however, when he had to do what he could to hide this physique from the camera, to keep in character.

Above, clockwise from top left: Stills from the Essanay films and the Mutual-Chaplin Specials: Chaplin with Eric Campbell in *The Rink*; as a street musician in *The Vagabond*; with Edna Purviance and Kitty Bradbury in *The Immigrant*; in drag for *A Woman*; with Ben Turpin in *His New Job*; in *The Tramp*; in *The Floorwalker*; as Mr Pest in *A Night in the Show*; as Darn Hosiery in *Burlesque on Carmen*; and with Edna Purviance and Leo White *In the Park*.

Above: Thomas Ince (in dark jacket), Chaplin, Mack Sennett, and D. W. Griffith (*far right*) at the Keystone Studio in 1915.

Opposite top: (*left to right*) Chaplin, John Jasper, Henry Bergman, Carl Robinson, Eric Campbell, Albert Austin, and Sydney Chaplin at the ground-breaking Chaplin Studios, October 1917.

Opposite below: Campbell, Marta Golden, Edna Purviance, and Chaplin in *The Adventurer*, 1917.

From Tramp to Hollywood Mogul

By the time he moved from Essanay in 1916 to the Mutual Film Corporation — to make what became known as the Mutual-Chaplin Specials — Chaplin had come close to exhausting the capabilities of the standard two-reel silent comedy, and many of the dozen Mutual-Chaplin films still have the look of filmed stage performances about them.

It took another change of studios before Chaplin the director began to approach the genius of Chaplin the comic. In June 1917, with Sydney again in attendance, Chaplin signed a contract with the First National Exhibitors' Circuit, a company formed by a group of well-

established movie theater owners. The signing bonus was now $75,000, and Chaplin's salary was to come out of the $125,000 budget allowed for each film. Chaplin built his own studio (at a cost of $34,000) and stayed with the company for over five years. In that time, however, he made only eight films, evidence that the madcap days of mass production were over, that he was taking time to complete each film, and that the films themselves were getting longer. Of the eight films, three were two-reelers, another three were three-reelers, but *Pay Day* ran to four reels, while *The Kid* (with six reels) ran for over an hour on screen.

It was Chaplin's good fortune to come into movies at a time when the industry was undergoing its first major revolution. In 1914, D. W. Griffith joined forces with Thomas Ince and Mack Sennett to create the Triangle Film Corporation. Griffith wrote the grammar of cinema with the films he made, and to his fellow pioneers he was "The Teacher of Us All". Less than two years after Chaplin's movie debut, Griffith released *Birth of a Nation*, the first American full-length feature film, and an astounding step forward in film-making. Chaplin was quick to learn.

P.417.

Left: The "Big Four" – (*left to right*)
Mary Pickford, D. W. Griffith,
Chaplin, and Douglas Fairbanks,
February 5, 1919.
Above: Chaplin (*on left*), with
Pickford and Fairbanks (*right*), and
another pioneer of early
Hollywood, Ernst Lubitsch, c. 1917.

"The One and Only"

Charlie Chaplin

His Signature

In his First Million Dollar Picture

"A DOG'S LIFE"

A "First National" Attraction

Above: Chaplin with Mutt, the dog who played the part of Scraps, in *A Dog's Life*, Chaplin's first film for First National, April 1918.

Left: A poster for the film. Chaplin described the film as having "an element of satire paralleling the life of a dog with that of a tramp". It was also a film in which he discarded any gags, no matter how funny, if they interfered with the logic of the story.

Above: A still from the attack sequence in *Shoulder Arms*, released in October 1918. The trenches were dug on rural wasteland not far from the center of Hollywood, and the exteriors were shot during a heat wave. The film took seventy-one days to shoot.

Chaplin Goes to War

When World War I broke out, Chaplin elected to stay in the United States. He shared the American view that it was strictly a European affair, expressed in the popular song *I Didn't Raise My Boy to Be a Soldier*. By 1917, however, when the US entered the war, Chaplin felt differently, and when invited to join a drive to sell Liberty Bonds, he embarked on a nationwide tour with Douglas Fairbanks and Mary Pickford.

Chaplin was not an experienced speaker and was still uncomfortable with words. His natural voice was thin and nasal, with little carrying power. As a music hall performer, he had been unable to make the spoken contact across the footlights which adds such intimacy and conspiracy between artist and audience. Nevertheless, he threw himself into the sales drive, bounding on to the makeshift stage and delivering a machine-gun barrage of words: "The Germans are at your door! We've got to stop them! And we will stop them if you buy Liberty Bonds! Remember, each bond you buy will save a soldier's life – a mother's son!…"

It worked. In New York alone, Fairbanks, Pickford, and Chaplin sold $2 million of bonds. But Chaplin found New York depressing, with "the ogre of militarism everywhere". He hated the "forced buoyancy" of military bands that accompanied the thousands of doughboys on their way to the docks to embark for France. Back in Los Angeles, he decided to make his own war film – *Shoulder Arms*. Cecil B. De Mille advised against it, saying: "It's dangerous at this time to make fun of the war", but Chaplin went ahead. He had wanted the film to be a five-reeler, but was dissatisfied with the result, and cut it drastically. Although he still was not satisfied with the film, it was a smash hit.

To, The "Chief",
yours for old
times sake...
Charlie Chaplin
Feb. 23rd. 1918.

The Tramp and the King

The first meeting between Chaplin and Douglas Fairbanks, the King of Hollywood, was arranged by Constance Collier, leading lady with Sir Herbert Beerbohm Tree's company. It took place at Fairbanks' Beverly Hills home. Both men were at first wary of each other, for they had little in common save a talent for making silent movies. Fairbanks was all for riding out into the wilds on horseback to greet the dawn; Chaplin preferred to greet it in bed with a beautiful woman. Nevertheless, the two became lifelong friends, and great admirers of each other's work. When Chaplin was considering throwing *Shoulder Arms* into the trash can, he showed the film to Fairbanks. In Chaplin's words: "From the beginning Fairbanks went into roars of laughter, stopping only for coughing spells… when it was over, his eyes were wet from laughing…"

Opposite: Chaplin and Jackie Coogan (*center*) receive a visit from Major General George Barnett (*on Chaplin's left*), Head of the US Marine Corps, on the set of *The Kid,* 1921.

Left: Chaplin prepares to fly from Croydon to Paris en route to the United States, October 5, 1921.

The Kid

The Kid took a year to shoot and another five months in post-production to complete, at a total cost of $500,000. It was worth every cent, a genuine masterpiece from the opening title, "A picture with a smile — and perhaps, a tear", to the closing scene when the Tramp and the Kid are finally reunited. For sheer emotional intensity, the only Chaplin film to match *The Kid* is perhaps *City Lights*. Chaplin threw his whole childhood into the movie — the years on the streets, imprisonment in the orphanage, the loss of his mother, the absence of his father, the very garrets and attics in which he lived as a child, the unfeeling authorities who broke up his family, even the loss of a child — for he began filming *The Kid* on July 31, 1919, only three weeks after the death of his own infant son. The movie premiere at Carnegie Hall, New York City, in 1921 was a triumph.

Above: (*left to right*) Hiram Abrams, President of United Artists; Dennis F. O'Brien; Mary Pickford; Mrs. Charlotte Pickford; Chaplin; Arthur Kelly; Fairbanks; and Joseph M. Schenck at the Pickford-Fairbanks Studio, 1924.
Opposite: Douglas Fairbanks Junior, Paul Whiteman, unknown, Chaplin, Fairbanks Senior, and two unknowns, c. 1925.

The Artists United

In 1919, Chaplin joined with D. W. Griffith, Mary Pickford, and Douglas Fairbanks to set up a distribution company – the United Artists Corporation. Griffith, Pickford, and Fairbanks saw the creation of United Artists as a way to finance their film-making and thereby keep a larger percentage of the profits from the films they made. Chaplin, however, had different ideas: "I never thought of United Artists as a money-making scheme," he said. "It was a way of distributing my films." A stubborn maverick, Chaplin irritated Fairbanks and Griffith until they died, and exasperated Pickford until he finally sold his stock in the company in 1955. Creatively, however, Chaplin's years with United Artists were among his finest. Over a period of twenty-four years he made eight films, two of which were among his greatest – *The Gold Rush* (1925) and *City Lights* (1931).

Above: Color poster for *The Gold Rush*, 1925. The idea for the film came one Sunday morning when Chaplin and Fairbanks were looking at stereoscopic pictures of the Klondike. Chaplin saw a potential theme, which was fleshed out when he read the story of the Donner tragedy, when stranded pioneers turned to cannibalism.

Above: Two stills from *The Gold Rush.* (*left*) The Lone Prospector arrives at the remote cabin; (*right*) Chaplin with Tom Murray as Black Larsen. Chaplin was determined that the film would be a success: "This next film must be an epic!" In the end, he said it was the film he wished to be remembered by.

Left: (*left to right*) Fairbanks; an unknown giant supporting the "Dwarf Sisters" Elizabeth and Helen; Margaret Hay; and Chaplin, September 1922.

Right: Alfred Reeves, Chaplin's manager, stands by a wall covered with French posters of Chaplin, c. 1925.

Above: Chaplin with the world
famous violinist Jascha Heifetz.
Chaplin was no mean violin player
himself, and his favorite recording
was that of Heifetz playing Max
Bruch's *Violin Concerto No. 1*.

Above: Witzel's portrait of Chaplin playing the violin in May 1928. Chaplin played left-handed, practising from four to six hours a day when in his late teens. He had ambitions to be a concert artist, but realized he would "never achieve excellence".

The Circus

In his *Autobiography*, Chaplin has nothing to say about *The Circus*, although it won him a Special Academy Award "For versatility and genius in acting, writing, directing, and producing" the film. Financially, *The Circus* was the seventh highest grossing film in cinema history, taking more than $3.8 million in 1928, the year of its release. It was made three years after *The Gold Rush,* and in the time between the two films Chaplin was seriously ill, married Lita Grey, and had two children, suffered the death of his mother, did battle with the IRS, traveled extensively, embarked on several affairs, and met a great many famous people. His temporary absence from the film studios came at an inappropriate time. A new revolution hit Hollywood: Warner Brothers' first talkie premiered on October 6, 1927, and was an instant success. By the time *The Circus* was premiered at the Mark Strand Theater, New York City, exactly four months later, it was already out of date.

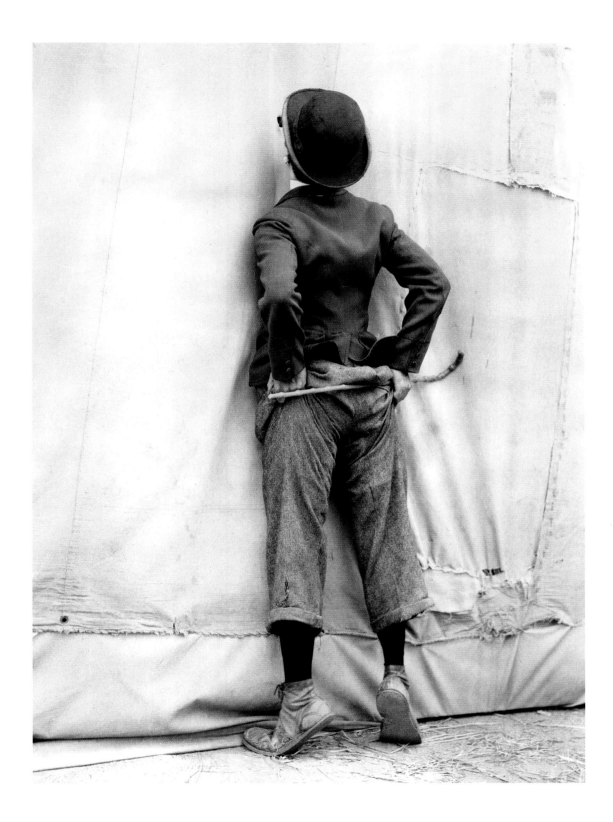

Above: On the set of *City Lights* in 1930 with (*left to right*) unknown, Randolph Churchill, Alfred Reeves, Wheeler Dryden, Chaplin, unknown, and Winston Churchill (*far right*). Chaplin met Winston Churchill several times – at Marion Davies's beach house, at Churchill's hotel in Los Angeles, and at Chartwell.

Opposite: Chaplin poses with a Charlie doll at the Chaplin Studios, 1922.

Above: Normand with Ralph Graves in Mack Sennett's 1923 comedy *The Extra Girl*.
Opposite above: Mabel Normand in 1926.
Opposite below: Normand in a scene from *What Happened to Rosa*, 1920. Like Chaplin, Normand found it hard to succeed in the theater, where her voice was too soft. She died of tuberculosis in 1930.
Previous page: Chaplin with the actress Muriel Harvey, c. 1917.

Charlie, Mack, and Mabel

Mabel Normand was twenty-one when she first met Chaplin. She had entered the film industry five years earlier, and had then embarked on a full-blooded affair with Mack Sennett who whisked her away to Keystone. Normand was actor, writer, comedian, and director, and it was she who recommended to Sennett that he hire Chaplin, and keep him on the payroll after an inauspicious start.

When Chaplin complained to Sennett that he detested working with Henry Lehrman, Sennett arranged for Normand to direct Chaplin's next film. In all, she directed Chaplin in four films and starred with him in a dozen, the penultimate being *Tillie's Punctured Romance* in December 1914. His attitude to her as a director may have been patronizing, but it is probable that they had an affair, although Chaplin makes no mention of this in his life story, *My Autobiography*.

"She was," he wrote, "extremely pretty, with large heavy-lidded eyes and full lips that curled delicately at the corners of her mouth… She was light-hearted and gay, a good fellow, kind and generous; and everyone adored her."

Left: Edna Purviance. "She was more than pretty," wrote Chaplin, "she was beautiful… It was inevitable that the propinquity of a beautiful girl like Edna would eventually involve my heart."

Above: Purviance wishes Chaplin good luck as he boards a train at Salt Lake Station, Los Angeles, on a nationwide whistle-stop tour selling Liberty Bonds during World War I.

Mildred Harris and the Little Mouse

It was while he was still romantically involved with Purviance, that Chaplin made the first of his two disastrous early marriages. His first and second wives were women of considerable spirit with large financial appetites.

Chaplin married for the first time in 1918. It was a shotgun wedding, for his seventeen-year-old bride (Mildred Harris) had told Chaplin she was pregnant. Chaplin knew that he risked criminal prosecution for sexual involvement with a minor, and decided to make an honest woman of her. But it was all a bluff; Harris was not pregnant.

Not surprisingly, after such an unpromising start, the marriage quickly began to fall apart. Harris and Chaplin did have a child, but tragically Norman Spencer Chaplin ("The Little Mouse") lived for only three days. They separated two months later, in Chaplin's words, "we were mis-mated". Within a year, Harris filed for divorce on the grounds of cruelty. Egged on by lawyers, she demanded a share in the profits of *The Kid* as part of the settlement. Chaplin was horrified. The film meant far more to him than his wife did. His lawyers went to work and persuaded Harris to

drop her demands, in return for which Chaplin would not contest the divorce action. Artistically and financially, Chaplin got what he wanted, but the scandal harmed his public image.

Following their divorce in 1920, Harris had a brief but high-profile affair with the then Prince of Wales. From then on, both her professional and private lives proceeded downhill, and in her late career she worked with the Three Stooges.

Opposite left: Mildred Harris applies make-up on the set of a 1923 picture, made after her divorce from Chaplin.

Opposite right: A portrait of Harris in 1925, the year in which her only surviving child was born.

Above: The gravestone of Norman Spencer Chaplin, "The Little Mouse".

Following pages left: Richard Brinsley Sheridan and his mother, Clare Consuelo Sheridan, artist and sculptor, with whom Chaplin had a brief affair in 1921. The photograph was taken when Sheridan arrived in the US for a lecture tour on her experiences in Soviet Russia.

Right: Peggy Hopkins (the name of her second husband) Joyce (the name of her fourth husband – she had six in all). She was the model for Chaplin's *A Woman of Paris*. For two weeks in 1922, Joyce and Chaplin were inseparable.

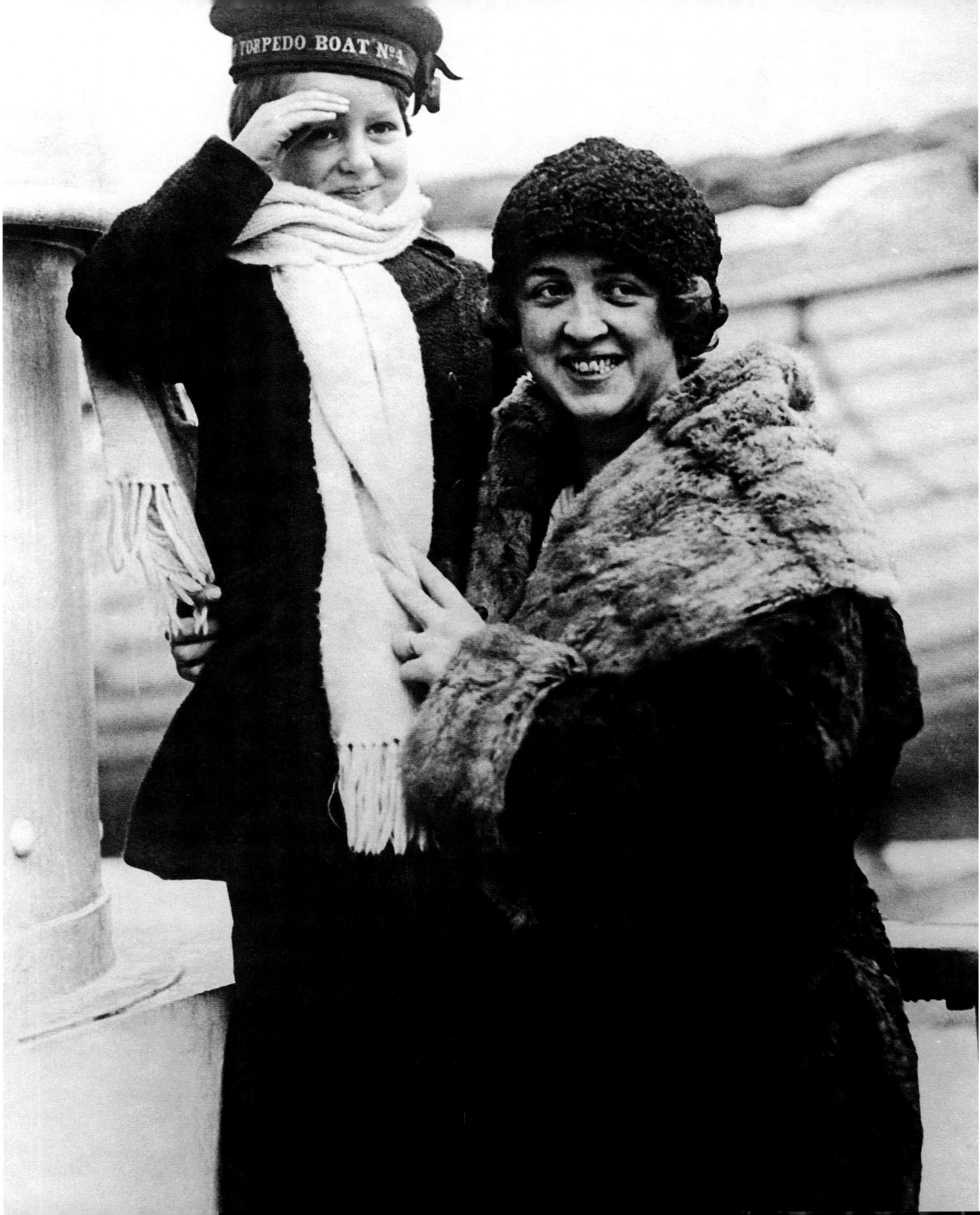
TORPEDO BOAT Nº4

The Roaring Twenties

Several of his partners have acknowledged Chaplin's considerable sexual appetite. But, as with so much of his psychological make-up, there appears to have been a polarization between the yin and yang of Chaplin's sex life. He wanted the yang of sex, but appears to have been frightened of its dark side, of venereal disease. In the first half of the 20th century, VD was still a terrifying scourge, and Chaplin took what seem today strange measures to protect himself from it. Louise Brooks, who had an affair with Chaplin when she was an eighteen-year-old dancer with the Ziegfeld Follies in 1925, described how

Chaplin would paint his penis with iodine as protection against the disease before having intercourse with her. The tragedy of his mother's insanity, caused by contracting syphilis at an early age, may well have preyed on Chaplin's mind, for when he left the arms of Brooks and returned to those of his second wife, he obsessively showered eight or ten times a day. At no time, however, did his fear of syphilis prevent him from doing his best to emulate the adventures of Don Juan and Casanova.

Chaplin was forthcoming about most of the loves in his life, but it is difficult to be sure just how many sexual partners

he had. In his autobiography, he wrote: "to gauge the morals of our family by ordinary standards would be like plunging a thermometer into boiling water". For his own part, he claimed to have slept with at least 2,000 women. He was neither proud of nor ashamed of this figure, which was probably an exaggeration, certainly no more than a rough guess. The list includes at least seven of his leading ladies – three of whom he married – several other famous movie stars, secretaries, artists and, when the mood was on him, almost any young woman that took his fancy.

Opposite: The actress Pola Negri on Santa Monica Beach, near Hollywood in 1925. Chaplin described their relationship as "exotic".
Left: A 1925 portrait of Louise Brooks. Chaplin managed to combine his affair with Brooks with a nervous breakdown.

Above: Marion Davies as Tina in *The Red Mill*, 1926.

Right: Davies in 1925. Chaplin described her as, to his surprise, "quite a comedienne, with charm and appeal", someone "who would have been a star in her own right without the Hearst cyclonic publicity."

Opposite: Chaplin and Merna Kennedy on the set of *The Circus* in 1928. Kennedy was still a teenager, Chaplin was nearing forty. Kennedy had been introduced to Chaplin by his second wife, Lita Grey. Within months, Grey filed for divorce from Chaplin on the grounds of his affair with Kennedy.

Charlie Takes a Risk

Between his first and second marriages, Chaplin slept with (among others): Clare Sheridan – widow, Communist, and cousin of Winston Churchill; Peggy Joyce; Pola Negri – who was probably having an affair with Rudolph Valentino at the same time; Georgia Hale; Merna Kennedy; and Marion Davies.

Chaplin first met Davies in his early Hollywood days, when she was already the mistress of William Randolph Hearst, the media mogul and model for *Citizen Kane*. The meeting was arranged by the novelist and screenwriter Elinor Glyn, and Chaplin was surprised and charmed by Davies's appeal: "She was quite a comedienne… and from that moment we struck up a great friendship".

It was a dangerous liaison. Hearst was a jealous and vicious man who hired private detectives to keep an eye on the comings and goings of his mistress – a woman thirty-four years his junior. Such was Hearst's reputation, a rumor circulated that he had shot and killed the movie producer Thomas Ince after discovering him in bed with Davies, believing him to be Chaplin.

Lita Grey

In 1924, Chaplin began an affair with Lillita MacMurray. She was a sixteen-year-old Hollywood hopeful, whom he had given a minor role in *The Kid*. He renamed her Lita Grey, and groomed her for the female lead in *The Gold Rush*. Grey became pregnant. Chaplin wanted her to have an abortion, and offered her $40,000 to marry someone else. Grey refused. By the time the shotgun wedding took place in Empalme, Mexico in November 1924, all affection between them had died.

Almost exactly two years later, Grey left Chaplin, taking with her the two children of the marriage. She immediately filed for divorce, on the grounds of Chaplin's adultery with a host of women. It was a bitterly acrimonious lawsuit. Grey initially accused Chaplin of seduction, statutory rape, sexual perversion, violence, and of threatening to kill her. Most of these charges were later withdrawn.

The divorce settlement cost Chaplin a record $825,000. He emerged from the proceedings bitter, exhausted, and white-haired, and plunged into a nervous breakdown. Many years later, he singled Grey out as the one woman in his life he had not loved.

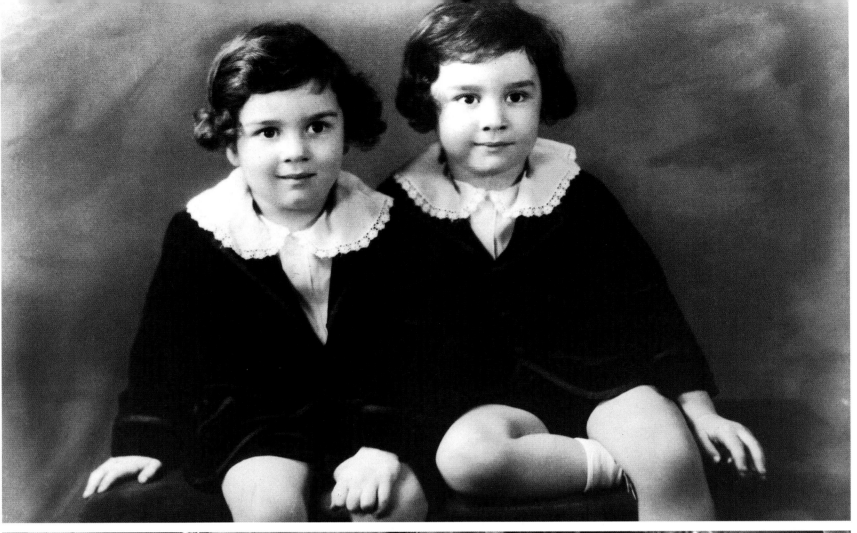

Opposite top: Sydney Earle Chaplin (*left*) and Charles Chaplin Junior.
Opposite below: Lita Grey (*far right*) with (*left to right*) Lillian Parker, Charles Chaplin Junior, W. E.Curry (Lita's grandfather), and Sydney Earle Chaplin.
Left: Charles Junior and Sydney Earle on the set of *Modern Times*, 1936.

The Final Settlement

Given Chaplin's peccadilloes, it was hardly surprising that Grey was given the custody of the children of their miserable marriage, but Chaplin's problems with Grey continued into the 1930s. In 1932, Chaplin felt compelled to go to court in an attempt to prevent Grey from allowing Charles Junior and Sydney Earle to appear in a film for the Fox Film Corporation. This time, the court found in Chaplin's favor.

From then on, Grey's life was a downward spiral. She entered into four more unhappy marriages, lost most of the money she had taken from Chaplin in the stock market collapse of 1929, became an alcoholic, and worked as a humble sales-clerk until the age of seventy-seven. She lived until 1995, outlasting all Chaplin's other wives.

With one exception, Chaplin never encountered much trouble with any of his mistresses, during or after an affair. No woman ever killed herself when he brought the relationship to an end, and no man ever threatened to kill him for stealing a woman. The exception, the rejected mistress who did cause trouble was Joan Barry, with whom Chaplin had a brief "fling" in 1942. When Chaplin ended the affair, Barry broke into his house, waving a gun and threatening to kill herself. She then leaked a story that she was pregnant with Chaplin's child to Hedda Hopper, one of the most powerful newspaper columnists in America. The American press roasted Chaplin, who never recovered his former popularity in the US.

The Tramp and His Libido

What emerges from the statistics (vital or not) relating to Chaplin's sexual partners, is that many were probably looking for an older man, a father figure. Oona O'Neill, Chaplin's fourth and last wife (thirty-six years his junior) used to call him "Pops". His first two wives (Mildred Harris and Lita Grey) were both only sixteen when Chaplin married them and, although his third wife (Paulette Goddard) was twenty-two when they married, the affair had begun four years earlier. With the exception of Clare Sheridan, all Chaplin's mistresses, lovers, and passing sexual partners were younger than he was, many of them were still teenagers, and some were illegally young. Chaplin never fell for or pursued the older woman.

Charlie Chaplin was a handsome man with a mighty sense of humour. As such, he was bound to be attractive to women long before he added fame and wealth to his list of attributes. He was also a man who craved love from women. This was not surprising, given that his own mother's love for him had been a stuttering affair, irregularly administered in dribs and drabs. But it is too simplistic to ascribe Chaplin's four marriages and innumerable affairs to a psychological yearning for the woman's care that he was denied as a child. There may well have been something special in the Chaplin genes – Darryl F. Zanuck, who worked with Sydney Chaplin in the 1920s, described Charlie's brother as "the greatest ladies man in Hollywood, better even than Errol Flynn".

Whatever lay at the root of Chaplin's seemingly insatiable lust, the names of four women stand out: Edna Purviance – with whom he remained friends for decades; Georgia Hale – who starred with him in *The Gold Rush*, whom Chaplin wanted for *The Circus*, and whom he considered for *City Lights*; Virginia Cherrill – the one leading lady who was not his mistress; and Paulette Goddard.

"My Little Baby"

Shortly after his return to Hollywood from his world tour in the early 1930s, Chaplin met and fell in love with a young dancer, actress, and Ziegfeld girl named Paulette Goddard. Like so many of Chaplin's partners, Goddard, too, was the product of a broken marriage. By Chaplin's standards, it was a happy and long-lasting affair that is generally reckoned to have graduated into marriage. However, some of the fog that hangs around so much of Chaplin's private life, attaches to his relationship with Goddard – as it does to Goddard's birth date, which is variously given as 1905, 1909, 1910, and 1911. Publicly, Chaplin claimed that he and Goddard were married in China in 1936 and

divorced in Mexico in 1942; privately, he is said subsequently to have told members of his family that he and Goddard were never married.

For once, there was mutual admiration in Chaplin's relationship with a woman. Goddard was bright, intelligent, and talented, as well as beautiful. In her eyes, Chaplin was not only "the greatest creator of films", but also "the most charming of men". "Nobody," she told a reporter for the *New York Times,* "was his equal." In a biography of Goddard, written by Julie Gilbert, there is a moving account of the last meeting between Goddard and Chaplin. It took place at a gala tribute to Chaplin held in the Lincoln Center in

1972, forty years after they had first met, thirty-two years after their amicable divorce. Goddard went up to Chaplin and greeted him with their customary "Hello, baby". Chaplin's eyes filled with tears. "My little baby," he said. "Yes," she replied, "your only little baby." He was then eighty-three, she was sixty-two. Goddard was clearly special in Chaplin's eyes. Describing their separation in his autobiography, he wrote: "The wrench naturally hurt, for it was hard cleaving eight years' association from one's life". Save for Oona O'Neill, no other woman meant as much to him as his little *gamine* from *Modern Times.*

Above, left to right: House photographer, Gene Lester captures Paulette Goddard and Chaplin at Ciro's nightclub, Hollywood, 1940. Paulette Goddard is flanked by Chaplin (*on left*) and the writer Konrad Bercovici at a Hollywood night out. Bercovici collaborated with Chaplin on the screenplay for *The Great Dictator*, but later sued Chaplin, alleging that he received neither due reward nor recognition. Ever the perfectionist, Chaplin puts the finishing touches to Goddard's hair on the set of *Modern Times*, 1935. Chaplin and Goddard with Olympic swimmer Duke Kahanamoku bid "aloha" to Honolulu, Hawaii, 1936.

Right: Chaplin (*right*) and Goddard with Tim Durant at the Brown Derby restaurant, 1935. At the time, it was rumored that Goddard was married to Durant.

CHAPTER 4

The Tramp and the Dictator

(1931-1940)

The Tramp and the Talkies

With the exception of Laurel and Hardy, few of the great silent film comedians rushed to embrace the coming of the "talkies". Many faded from the scene altogether or were reduced to playing bit parts in sound films. Once the big change came, Chaplin made only three more Little Tramp movies: *City Lights* (1931), *Modern Times* (1936), and *The Great Dictator* (1940). They were all hugely successful, a tribute to Chaplin's genius, for they were all anachronisms – silent films made in the era of sound.

Chaplin never wanted to make sound films. He feared that adding a spoken soundtrack would slow the pace of his comedy, destroy the universality of its appeal, and kill the beauty and the subtlety of his art. Moreover, he believed that his next project – *City Lights* – would be "an ideal silent picture".

Early in its production, Chaplin's mother died in a Los Angeles hospital. She had moved to the States in 1921, and her last few years had been painful and unhappy ones, racked with physical pain and mental anguish as her insanity took hold. Although her mental illness had made her a remote figure (in his life), he mourned her death.

Previous page: A 1936 French-produced postcard for what many consider Chaplin's greatest film, *Modern Times*.
Above and opposite: Two studies of Chaplin during the 1930s, a decade that saw him reach the pinnacle of his career.

Above: Douglas Fairbanks Junior,
Mary Pickford, and Chaplin at a
United Artists Conference in 1930.
Fairbanks Junior was Pickford's step
son; his mother was Anna Beth Sully,
first wife of Douglas Fairbanks Senior.

Above: A view of Chaplin's Beverly
Hills mansion in the late 1920s.
When Chaplin first visited Beverly
Hills, he described it as looking like
"an abandoned real estate
development".

Above: *(left to right)* Harry Myers,
as the Eccentric Millionaire, and Allan
Garcia, as the Butler, entertain the
Tramp in a scene from *City Lights*.
The film was Chaplin's personal
favorite of all the films he made.

Left: The Tramp's first meeting with the Blind Flower Girl. Virginia Cherrill was herself visually handicapped, being extremely short-sighted. She was briefly married to Cary Grant, and later to the 9th Earl of Jersey.

City Lights

Though ill for much of the time, Chaplin never ceased to demand perfection from himself and the entire cast and crew during the making of *City Lights*. Chaplin's attention to detail was such that it took nearly 350 takes of the scene in which the Tramp and the Flower Girl meet for the first time before he was satisfied – a world record. He locked himself away for hours at a time when he felt the film needed another gag, another twist of the plot, or another turn of the emotional screw. He drove himself so hard that production had to be halted for a month when he became ill.

In the end, the effort was worthwhile. Critics and fellow film-makers had nothing but praise for the film; the public flocked to see it, and the film made a profit of $5 million. *City Lights* remains one of the most praised films in the history of movies. The writer and critic James Agee described the final scene in *City Lights* as "…enough to shrivel the heart to see… it is the greatest piece of acting and the highest moment in movies…".

Above: A still from the
subsequently abandoned boxing
sequence in *City Lights*. Chaplin's
method of film-making, where gags
and ideas were added during
shooting meant that many scenes
were cut entirely. At one time, *City
Lights* included a fantasy sequence
where the Tramp saw himself as a
Ruritanian prince.

Above: The giant Tramp on the façade of the Dominion Cinema, Tottenham Court Road, during the London run of *City Lights,* 1931. Three performances a day was nothing. At the George M. Cohan Theater in Los Angeles, the first screening of *City Lights* started at 9am, the last at midnight.

Charlie and the Celebrities

When Chaplin returned to London in 1931, after the making of *City Lights*, he was even more popular than before. Not only did the public love him, he was now moving in the highest circles. Chaplin's *entrée* into London society was initially provided by Sir Philip Sassoon MP, reckoned to be London's most eligible bachelor. Sassoon invited Chaplin to dine at his town house in Park Lane, and to weekend with him at his Port Lympne estate in Kent. He also took him to lunch at the House of Commons, where Chaplin met Lady Astor. She, in turn, invited Chaplin to lunch at No. 1, St. James's Square, where

he met George Bernard Shaw, John Maynard Keynes, and David Lloyd George. In Chaplin's words: "It was like stepping into the Hall of Fame at Madame Tussaud's." The luncheon was a huge success, culminating in Lady Astor cramming a set of comedy protruding teeth into her mouth, and giving an imitation of a Victorian lady addressing an equestrian club.

One meeting led to another, and within the next three weeks, Chaplin met the Prime Minister, Ramsay MacDonald; his old friend Winston Churchill, who invited him to spend a weekend at Chartwell, where Churchill

taught Chaplin how to build a brick wall; Mahatma Gandhi; the author H. G. Wells; the painter Alfred Munnings; Harold Laski, Professor of Political Science at the London School of Economics; and the Duke and Duchess of York – later King George VI and Queen Elizabeth.

At short notice, Chaplin was invited to take part in a charity Command Performance at the London Palladium. The invitation arrived when he was recovering from his London visit at Juan-les-Pins, in the South of France. Instead of accepting, he sent a cheque for £200 made out to the charity concerned. His innocent action caused great offence.

Opposite: (*left to right*) Lady
Milbanke; Chaplin; Edward, Prince of
Wales (later the Duke of Windsor);
and the Duchess of Sutherland. They
were attending a Halloween
Celebration Dinner in London.
Above: Chaplin (*center*) flanked by
Albert and Elsa Einstein at the world
premiere of *City Lights* at the George
M. Cohan Theater, Los Angeles, January
30, 1931. The poignant ending of the
film reduced Einstein to tears.

Above: Chaplin visits one of his old haunts, south of the river, during his stay in London for the British premiere of *City Lights*, 1931. As in 1921, he was given a hero's welcome. "The world was an entertainment," he wrote, with childlike enthusiasm, "The performance started first thing in the morning."

Above: Chaplin strolls along the Thames Embankment, London, September 21, 1931. Ten years earlier, he had noted derelicts sleeping rough there, now they were gone. Chaplin stayed at the Carlton Hotel: "The saddest thing I can imagine is to get used to luxury. Each day I stepped into the Carlton was like entering a golden paradise."

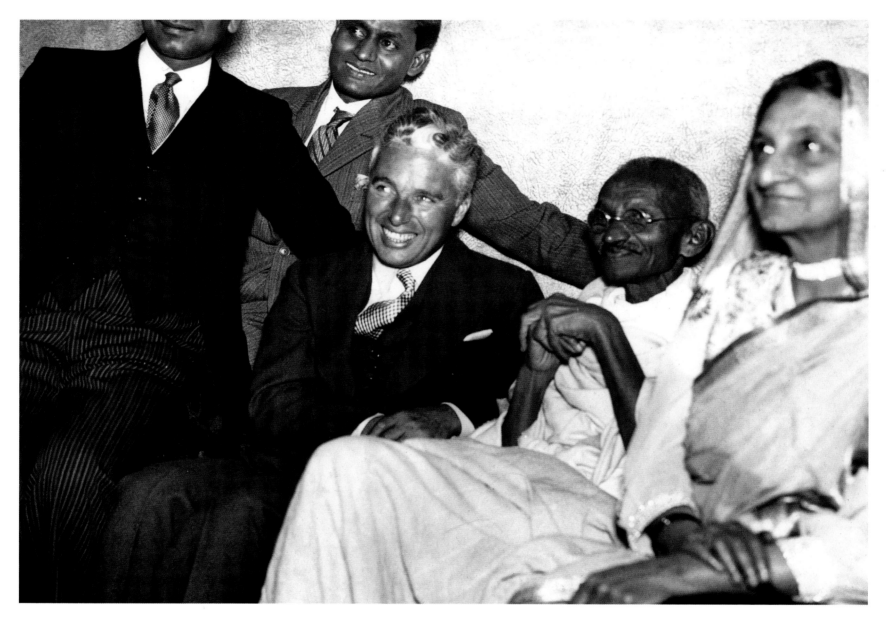

Above: Chaplin visits Gandhi at the house of Dr. Katial in Beckton Road, Canning Town, in the East End of London, September 22, 1931. They discussed factory assembly lines. Gandhi's abhorrence of such things gave Chaplin some of his ideas for the factory sequence in *Modern Times*.

Above: Chaplin in London 1931, outside the home of Lady Nancy Astor in St. James's Square. (*left to right*) Amy Johnson, the pioneer aviator who had recently completed her record flight from London to Japan; Chaplin; Lady Astor; and George Bernard Shaw.

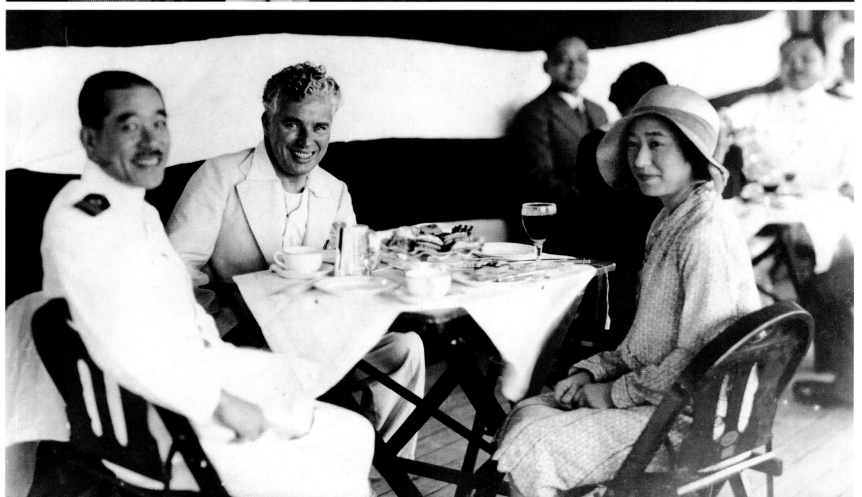

Charlie's Travels

As soon as it was clear that *City Lights* was going to be a smash hit on both sides of the Atlantic, Chaplin took an extended holiday. He went first to France and Germany, passed up an invitation from the Duke of Alba to visit Spain, on seeing newspaper headlines "Revolution in Spain", and went instead to Vienna and Venice. After a return trip to London, where he met the Prince of Wales, Chaplin and his brother Sydney set sail for Japan, via Suez, the Red Sea, Singapore, and Bali.

The visit to Japan was marred by a strange and frightening incident. Chaplin fell foul of a gangster and pornographer who was linked to an ultra-nationalist, right-wing, anti-American group called The Black Dragon. The group had a vague plan to murder Chaplin, whom they believed was regarded as "the darling of the capitalist class", while he was taking tea with the Japanese Prime Minister. Luckily for Chaplin, they abandoned this plan, although the Prime Minister was indeed later assassinated.

Opposite above: Sydney Chaplin (*second from left*) and Chaplin (*fourth from left*) meet with Japanese Sumo wrestlers, 1932.
Opposite below: Chaplin takes tea with Mrs Seibei Mogi on board the *SS Suwa Maru,* while sailing from Shanghai to Singapore with Paulette Goddard, on a later trip to Asia in March 1936.
Above: With brother Sydney (*third from left*) in a traditional Japanese tea house, 1932.

A Tramp of the Left

In 1934, Chaplin published a collection of essays entitled *A Comedian Sees the World*. Material for the book had come from Chaplin's sixteen-month world tour following the release of *City Lights,* a time when the Great Depression was biting deep in Europe and the US. Wherever he went, Chaplin saw all around him the twin evils of unemployment and exploitation. He was appalled and, at the end of his tour, Chaplin began to put together ideas for a new film, a comedic and satirical critique of the modern industrial system, which was to expose the slavery of the human labor force in the machine age,

the spying supervision of workers by management, and the collusion of police and state authorities in the oppression of the poor.

Chaplin's previous silent greats had at their heart personal stories of distinct individuals, struggling against poverty. *Modern Times* was to be different – a fable about mass poverty, for all times and all people. For the first time in a Chaplin film, hero and heroine represented an entire class of society. The Tramp and the *gamine* represented millions then involved in all the horrors of the Depression.

Above: A group of young boys visit Chaplin on the set of *Modern Times*, 1935. The original caption for this picture described the boys as young "statists", those who believe in the doctrine of giving central government control over economic planning and policy.

Above: Chaplin, in make-up, prepares a camera shot while working on *Modern Times*. As in his previous films, Chaplin produced, directed, scripted, and edited the film, as well as composing a full music score.

The Making of Modern Times

The filming of *Modern Times* began on October 11, 1934 and was completed on August 30, 1935 — a relatively short time span for a Chaplin feature film. It was not a truly silent film. Although Chaplin ultimately rejected the idea of using dialogue, he did add music, sound effects, a tiny clip of speech from the Tramp (in the prison sequence), and some gibberish sung by the Tramp as a singing waiter in a restaurant. It was a brave decision to leave it at that. By the time *Modern Times* was premiered at the Rivoli Theater, New York City on February 5, 1936, movie fans were used to all the genres created by the "talkies": musicals, wisecracking comedies, and tough guy verbal exchanges between cops and villains. Chaplin could have lost a lot of money but, though not as successful financially as *City Lights*, *Modern Times* made enough to bring in a reasonable profit.

Above: The Tramp is about to be sucked into the (foam rubber) machine – a still from *Modern Times*.

Right: Chaplin and Paulette Goddard, as the Tramp and the *gamine*, set up home together.

Left: Chaplin with his fifteen-year-old son, Sydney Earle, in 1940. Sydney had a troubled and unhappy childhood. By the time he was sixteen he had been expelled from three boarding schools.

The Coming of the Great Dictator

The end of *Modern Times* shows the Tramp once again shuffling down a country road, heading toward the setting sun and away from the camera. But this time he is not alone; the *gamine* is at his side. The inference is clear: the Tramp's search for a soul-mate, a playmate, and a lover is over; the odyssey that began in 1915 with the old Essanay two-reeler of *The Tramp*, has come to a happy ending.

Chaplin certainly intended that his Tramp would henceforth rest in peace. He had formally announced the Tramp's retirement in 1937. *The New York Times* had even printed a farewell to the little clown: "Goodbye, Charlot.

Pleasant dreams." But Alexander Korda (film producer and one of Chaplin's partners at United Artists) pointed out to Chaplin the incredible physical similarity between the Tramp and Adolf Hitler. Couldn't Chaplin use this resemblance to his advantage in a film which revolved around the similarity? Whether or not the Tramp did return, as the little Jewish barber in *The Great Dictator,* Chaplin's make-up was exactly the same for both characters, and their costumes were remarkably similar. The characterization was also much the same – the combination of cheek and humility.

But Chaplin observed with growing concern the rise of extreme nationalism in Europe, and saw that a film about a present day dictator would be both challenging and apposite. He was also personally stung by Nazi anti-Semitic propaganda that described him as being a "little Jewish tumbler, as disgusting as he is boring". In September 1938, while British Prime Minister Neville Chamberlain scurried back and forth between London and Bavaria seeking a treaty with Hitler, Chaplin began work on the script of *The Great Dictator.*

Above: Hollywood Stars gather for a coast-to-coast radio broadcast. Back row (*left to right*) unknown, Douglas Fairbanks Senior, Joseph M. Schenk; front row (*left to right*) Dolores del Rio, John Barrymore, Chaplin, D.W. Griffith, and Norma Talmadge. The photograph came from the Publicity Director of Joseph M. Schenk Enterprises, but makes no mention as to why the faces of Fairbanks, Schenk, and Griffith were cut-outs, pasted on to the photograph.

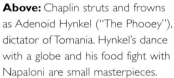 Chaplin struts and frowns as Adenoid Hynkel ("The Phooey"), dictator of Tomania. Hynkel's dance with a globe and his food fight with Napaloni are small masterpieces.

A Message to the World

There were plenty who criticised *The Great Dictator* for its message and its political stance. Some saw the film as an attack on capitalism. Americans who wished to keep the United States out of the war, disliked its call to arms. It also aroused the ever-present anti-Semitism that was directed at Chaplin throughout his career. Many thought he was a Jew. He wasn't, but had trained himself not to say that he wasn't, for he believed that if he did so he too would be guilty of anti-Semitism. Ironically, *The Great Dictator* managed to offend both Fascists and supporters of democracy.

Despite this, the film was Chaplin's most successful in financial terms. It cost $1.5 million to make, but grossed $5 million in takings. It was praised by many critics, endorsed by President Roosevelt, and was warmly received in Britain – a country that had threatened to ban the film in the days of appeasement. It was banned throughout Fascist-occupied Europe, in some South American countries, and initially banned by the Irish Film Classification Office.

Although *The Great Dictator* was nominated for five Academy Awards – Best Picture, Best Actor, Best Supporting Actor, Best Original Screenplay, and Best Original Score – none of the nominations graduated to an award. Perhaps the closing sermon was just too much. In the words of the novelist John O'Hara: "… no matter how deeply Chaplin may feel what he wrote and says, he is not a good preacher…".

When Chaplin heard that Hitler had seen *The Great Dictator*, he said: "I'd give anything to know what he thought of it". Sadly, the worst dictator did not share his reaction to the film with the rest of the world.

Above: Paulette Goddard and
Chaplin at the world premiere of
The Great Dictator, at the Capitol
Theater, New York City, October 15,
1940. The man with his left hand on
the microphone stand is Ed Sullivan.

CHAPTER 5

Charlie's Last Bow

(1940-1960)

"Fighting for My Liberty"

Chaplin made only four more films after *The Great Dictator*. The first of these was *Monsieur Verdoux*. Orson Welles had suggested that Chaplin make a film about the French serial killer Henri Desiré Landru, better known as "Bluebeard". Chaplin took up the idea, and created the suave and cynical *Monsieur Verdoux* ("Mister Soft Worm"), a man who murdered women and burnt their bodies in his incinerator.

There was trouble from the start. The Motion Picture Producers and Distributors of America refused to approve the film, labeling it "unacceptable". In script, casting, set design, camera angles, music, and every aspect of the film, Chaplin had his way, but his ignorance of modern film technology caused the film to fall way behind schedule. The result was that, when the film was completed, Chaplin had a sub-standard film on a risky subject with a message that was hardly likely to find favor in the land that had been his home since 1910. Sixty years on, there is little that shocks in *Monsieur Verdoux*, but members of the American Legion and the Catholic War Veterans condemned it and picketed cinemas where it was shown. Chaplin fell back on his habitual love for his own work: "Frankly, I enjoy my comedies more than the audience".

The film premiered at a time when the Truman Doctrine (aimed at stemming the spread of Communism) had just come into force, and when the House Un-American Activities Committee was in full swing. Chaplin did what he could to promote the film, but it flopped in the United States. With commercial failure and political disfavor, Chaplin virtually wrote his own deportation order with *Monsieur Verdoux*.

Oona

For Chaplin, by far the best thing to come out of the 1940s was his marriage to Oona O'Neill. They first met in 1942, while Chaplin was embroiled in the unpleasant paternity lawsuit brought against him by Joan Barry. They were married within months, and immediately set about producing the family that figured so prominently in Chaplin's life. More than twenty years later, Chaplin rhapsodized on his love for O'Neill: "I have the good fortune to be married to a wonderful wife… As I live with Oona, the depth and beauty of her character are a continual revelation to me… a sudden wave of love and admiration comes over me for all that she is – and a lump comes into my throat…" She had come into his life in time to comfort and support him through a period when Chaplin was under attack professionally and politically.

Above: Chaplin's fingerprints are taken by George Rossini (*right*) of the US Marshal's Office, following Chaplin's arrest for allegedly violating the Mann Act, February 14, 1944. Looking on is Chaplin's attorney Jerry Giesler. Press photographers barged their way into the office to get the picture, almost certainly with the Marshal's connivance.
Opposite: Two stills from *Monsieur Verdoux*: (*top*) Verdoux with Annabella Bonheur (played by Martha Raye), the woman who keeps slipping through his fingers; (*below*) Verdoux with the Streetwalker, played by Marilyn Nash.

Above: Scenes from *Limelight*. (*clockwise from top left*) Buster Keaton and Chaplin; Claire Bloom as the young dancer Terry, and Chaplin; Sydney Earle Chaplin as Neville, and Claire Bloom; Chaplin as Calvero the Clown; (*left to right*) Oona, Chaplin, Bloom, and Sydney Chaplin at the London film premiere of *Limelight*, September 24, 1952; and three manifestations of Chaplin as Calvero.

The Émigré Family

In September 1952, Chaplin, Oona, and their children boarded the *Queen Elizabeth* and set sail for England. On the second day out, Chaplin's press assistant, Harry Crocker, received a cable. It stated that Chaplin was to be barred from the United States and that, before he could re-enter the country he would have to go before an Immigration Board of Inquiry to answer questions relating to his politics and what was described as his "moral turpitude".

Chaplin's reaction was strong: "I would like to have told them that the sooner I

was rid of that hate-beleaguered atmosphere the better, and that I was fed up with America's insults and moral pomposity." He held back much of his bitterness, however. By the time he reached London and received his customary hero's welcome, he felt better. Two years later, Oona loyally renounced her own American citizenship. Twenty years were to pass before Chaplin returned to the United States.

Opposite: Chaplin and family arrive at Southampton on board the *Queen Elizabeth*, September 23, 1952. (*left to right*) Geraldine, Josephine, Chaplin, Victoria, Michael, and Oona.

Above: Crowds greet Chaplin's arrival at London's Waterloo Station on board the boat train from Southampton, September 1952.

Above: The Chaplin family arrives at the Odeon Theatre, Leicester Square, London for the premiere of *Limelight*, October 16, 1952 – (*left to right*) Josephine, Chaplin, Michael, Victoria, and Oona Chaplin.

Opposite: Chaplin, newly arrived in the village, is invited to attend the beginning of the wine harvest at Villette, near Lausanne, Switzerland, October 8, 1953.

Above: A scene from Chaplin's 1957 film *A King in New York* – King Shahdov (Chaplin) takes instruction from the director of a TV commercial (Sid James) (*far right*).
Opposite: Chaplin tickles the ivories at La Reine Jeanne, home of his friend Paul Louis Weiller, at Bornes-les-Mimosas in the south of France, 1957.

Work and Play

Chaplin's return to Europe in 1952 offered more than mere relief from political persecution and legal prosecution. In London, especially, he was back among those who genuinely loved him, where he was famous rather than notorious. Although he criticized the post-war West End, in his eyes "now adulterated by American gimcracks, lunch counters, hot-dog stands and milk bars", Chaplin wanted Oona to fall in love with London, and was deeply grateful when she did.

Wherever he went, Chaplin was hailed as a celebrity, mobbed by crowds, and courted by the media and the Establishment. He dined at the House of Lords and mixed with cabinet ministers. "In Paris," he wrote, "we were received like conquering heroes." He lunched at the Elysée Palace with President Vincent Auriol, and was made an Officer of the Legion of Honor. He and Oona were guests of honor at the *Comédie-Française*. He lunched with Picasso and Jean-Paul Sartre. In Rome, he was decorated by Luigi Einaudi, President of Italy.

With so much goodwill surrounding him, it was simply a matter of choosing where in Europe he would settle down.

A King in New York

Chaplin made *A King in New York* at Shepperton Studios, London, in 1957. As usual, he wrote, directed, produced, starred in the film, and composed the full musical score. The film's plot was simple, and to the point. King Igor Shahdov, a recently deposed and penniless European monarch, arrives in New York seeking a new life. He befriends a young anarchist, falls foul of the US political system, is branded a Communist, and is summoned to appear before the House Un-American Activities Committee. Making the film allowed Chaplin to take humorous revenge on those who had harassed him over the previous ten or more years.

The film was successful in Europe, but was not released in the United States until 1970. For Chaplin's ten-year-old son Michael – who played the part of Rupert Macabee, the young anarchist – it was the happiest part of his childhood: "It was the first time I felt I had shared something with my father. He worked with me, rehearsed my lines and directed me. We were close for a short while…"

Opposite: A scene from *A King in New York*: King Shahdov's finger becomes stuck in the nozzle of a fire hose, leading to the drenching of a session of HUAC.

Above: Chaplin rehearses the studio orchestra prior to recording part of the music soundtrack for *A King in New York*, at the Palais de la Mutualité in Paris, 1957.

Left: Oona, Michael, and Chaplin arrive at London Airport for the world premiere of *A King in New York*, September 9, 1957.

Below: Chaplin and his son Michael on the terrace of the Manoir de Ban, Switzerland, c1957.

Left: The Chaplin family on holiday at Cap Ferrat, July 15, 1957 — (*left to right in top picture*) Oona, Geraldine (12 years old), Chaplin, Eugene (3), Michael (11), Victoria (6), and Josephine (8).

A New Home

The wandering Chaplins finally settled at the Manoir de Ban, Corsier, near Vevey, Switzerland. Here, between 1953 and 1962, Oona gave birth to two more sons and two more daughters, bringing their own number of children to eight — ten in all for Chaplin, with his sons from his marriage to Lita Grey. And here, the Chaplins entertained the great and the good, from Nehru to Noël Coward, from Truman Capote to the Queen of Spain.

It was the idyllic rural existence that Monsieur Verdoux had championed, and Chaplin devoted the last few lines of *My Autobiography* to the home he loved: "Thirty-seven acres," wrote Chaplin, "with an orchard which produces large black cherries, delicious green plums, apples and pears; and a vegetable garden that grows strawberries and wonderful asparagus and corn…"

Opposite: A new Chaplin meets the movie camera for the first time. (*left to right*) Chaplin, Eugene, Oona with recently arrived baby Jane, Josephine, Victoria, Michael, and Geraldine, at the Manoir de Ban, May 1957.

Public Father

Chaplin published his autobiography in 1964. His oldest child (Charles Spencer Chaplin Junior) was then thirty-two years old, his youngest (Christopher James Chaplin) was just two. Chaplin's early experience of life as a parent had been an unhappy and stuttering affair. His first child – the Little Mouse – had died when only a few days old. Charles Junior and Sydney Earle, his sons by Lita Grey, became estranged from him early in life. Not until Geraldine Chaplin was born in 1944 did Chaplin have the opportunity to show that he could be a good father.

It was Oona's children who were the subjects of the hundreds of pictures of Chaplin family life in the 1950s, 1960s, and 1970s. In these pictures, printed in newspapers and magazines around the world, Chaplin is always smiling, happy, seemingly devoted to, and thoroughly engaged with his children. The powerful image is of a man who is giving his children the fatherly love and care that he never had from his own father; their experience of childhood in the grounds of the Manoir de Ban was to be far removed from Chaplin's own miserable

childhood on the streets of south-east London back in the 1880s and 1890s.

Birthdays were great occasions, with all the trappings – presents, food, songs and laughter, pretty clothes – especially if there was a camera in sight. Christmas was an immense celebration. "My mother," wrote Michael Chaplin in his own autobiography, "would always put out a big tree in the house and we'd surround it with beautifully wrapped gifts." Smiling servants brought in beautifully prepared food. Scrooge was apparently nowhere to be seen.

Private Father

But the past kept getting in the way, especially at Christmas time. Chaplin, who had never experienced a happy Christmas in his childhood, loathed Christmas, and made a point of reminding his family each year that it was little more than an obscene consumer feast. The family posed for the world's cameras, but it was a public performance of a fairy tale.

Given Chaplin's lifelong attraction to young women, it is perhaps not surprising that he related more easily to his daughters than to his sons. He was also more relaxed when engaged in filming with his children – with Michael in *A King in New York*, and with Geraldine in *A Countess from Hong Kong* – although he took exception to Sydney's flirtation with Claire Bloom while making *Limelight*.

Geraldine Chaplin has written fondly of her father, whom she remembers as "a most remarkable man… with more energy than his children…". Michael Chaplin's memories of life with his father, however, suggest that Chaplin was emotionally repressed as a family man: "The old guy terrified the life out of me sometimes".

Opposite: Geraldine Chaplin and her father at the Manoir de Ban on the occasion of Chaplin's 70th birthday. In 1992, she played the part of her grandmother (Chaplin's mother, Lily Harley) in the biopic *Chaplin*.

Above: Members of the Chaplin family gather to celebrate his 70th birthday at the Manoir de Ban, April 17, 1959 – (*left to right*) Geraldine, Sydney, Josephine, Michael, Jane, Oona, and Chaplin.

Above: Chaplin looks on while his daughter Victoria performs a special piano sonatina to celebrate her father's birthday, April 19, 1960. The performance was a success.

Opposite: An airport photo of Chaplin and Oona in happy mood at the time of the making of *A Countess from Hong Kong*. The film was not a success, nor was it a happy time for those involved.

Rec

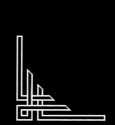

Previous page: A portrait of
Chaplin in a reflective mood in his
mid-eighties, c. 1974.
Above: The annual Chaplin Easter
Holiday in Ireland, fishing on one of
the Killarney lakes. Chaplin loved it,
but not all of his family were of the
same mind.

Above: Chaplin with the historian Professor George Ostrogorsky on the day that they both received their Honorary Doctorates at the University of Oxford, June 26, 1962. In the parade, directly behind Chaplin, was Dean Rusk, US Secretary of State. The crowd called out "Good old Charlie"; nobody rooted for Rusk.

Above: Another Christmas, another baby… (*left to right*) Eugene, Chaplin with Jane on his lap, Geraldine, Oona with baby Annette, Michael (*at rear*), Victoria, and Josephine, at the Manoir de Ban, December 1959.

Left: And two and a half years later, at the Mont-Choisi Clinic, Lausanne, Switzerland, a delighted Chaplin holds his latest and last baby, Christopher James, July 14, 1962.

Above: The Chaplin family pose for their 1964 Christmas Card picture – (*left to right on sofa*) Christopher, Oona, and Chaplin; (*left to right behind*) Annette, Jane, Eugene, Victoria, and Josephine. Chaplin's *My Autobiography* had just been published. It was translated into twenty-five languages.

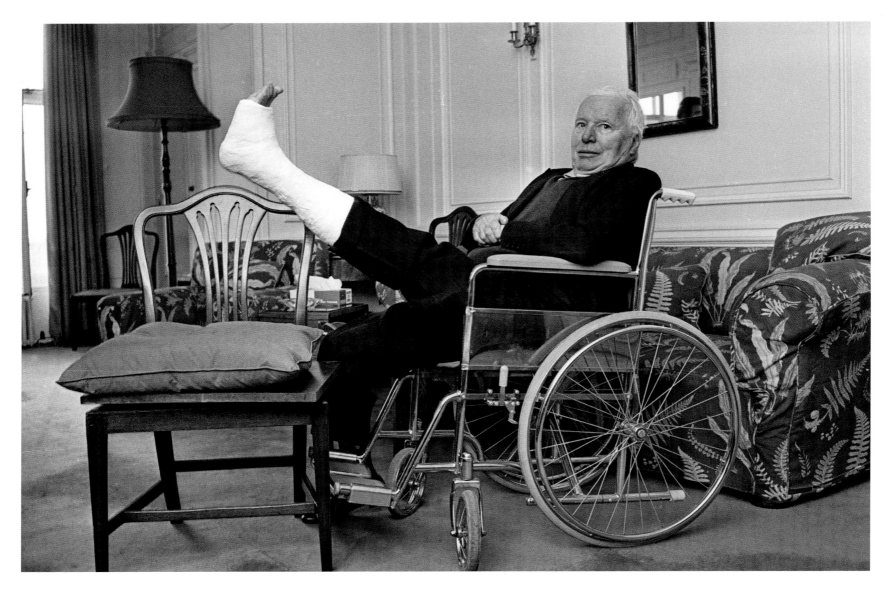

Above: Chaplin with a broken
ankle, caused by a fall at Pinewood
Studios, October 1966. Oona was
on set every day, trying to calm
things down. She later recalled:
"Once Charlie broke his ankle,
things became difficult… it did not
improve the nervous tension."

Above: An informal picture of Oona and Chaplin, taken during the filming of *A Countess from Hong Kong*, February 1966. With four Chaplins in the cast (Sydney Earle, Geraldine, Josephine, and Chaplin himself), it needed all Oona's care and patience to maintain the peace.

Above left: Chaplin with his sixteen-year-old daughter Josephine on the set at Pinewood while filming *A Countess from Hong Kong*, February 1966. Josephine had a bit part in the film.

Above right: Chaplin and Sophia Loren during the filming of *A Countess from Hong Kong*, April 1966.

Opposite: Two on-set shots of Chaplin and the film's male star, Marlon Brando, February 14, 1966. It was not a happy professional relationship: Brando's acting method and Chaplin's directorial style were incompatible, and Chaplin had originally wanted Sean Connery for the part. Brando described Chaplin as: "Probably the most sadistic man I'd ever met. He was an egotistical tyrant and a penny-pincher..."

Opposite above: Chaplin and Sophia Loren on the set at Pinewood Studios on Chaplin's seventy-seventh birthday, April 16, 1966.

Opposite below: A family group on the same set. (*back row, left to right*) Victoria, Elyane (a friend), Josephine, Chaplin; (*front row, left to right*) Marlon Brando, Loren with Annette on her knee, and Oona.

Above: Chaplin and Geraldine take the floor at L'Opéra in Paris during a Gala organized in his honor to celebrate the opening of *A Countess from Hong Kong*, January 1967. The great movie comedian W. C. Fields once described Chaplin as the best ballet dancer that ever lived.

Right: The seven-tiered cake to celebrate Chaplin's 77th birthday at Pinewood Studios, April 16, 1966. (*left to right*) Jospehine, Chaplin, Victoria, Oona, Sophia Loren, Sydney Earle, and Tippi Hedren with her daughter, Melanie Griffith.

Below: Chaplin tips his hat to locals in London's Old Kent Road while revisiting old haunts during the filming of *A Countess from Hong Kong*, 1966.

Above: Josephine Chaplin marries Greek businessman Nikolas Sistovaris at the Greek Orthodox Church, Lausanne, Switzerland, June 23, 1969. (*front row, left to right*) Nikolas Sistovaris and Josephine, Oona, Geraldine, and Chaplin.

Right: In the summer of 1971, Chaplin and Oona took a holiday on their own in Scotland, leaving their younger children (Christopher 9, Annette 12, and Jane 14) with their nannies at the Manoir de Ban. Here, Oona and Chaplin enjoy a place in the sun, July 21, 1971.

A King in Semi-retirement

Chaplin was getting olc. He still had his beloved Oona, and he still had his young family, but many friends, colleagues, and relations had gone. In 1957 his half-brother Wheeler Dryden died. The following year, Edna Purviance died of cancer, at the age of 62. He had kept her last letter, written a few weeks before her death – "and so the world grows young," he wrote, "and youth takes over". Others followed: his brother Sydney in 1965; Rollie Totheroh, his top cameraman for decades in 1967; and his oldest child, Charles Junior, in 1968.

But Chaplin had no thoughts of retiring. At the age of 75 he believed:

"My life is more thrilling today than ever it was. I am in good health and still creative and have plans to produce more pictures…"

He worked diligently on scripts and ideas for new films, with a daily routine that began with a swim in the outdoor pool, followed by breakfast with Oona, work in his library till lunch, then back to work till five, a game of tennis, a steam bath, a gin and tonic, dinner at 6.45 pm, and then more work. It was a busy schedule for a man in his seventies.

The Prodigal's Return

In the 1970s both Chaplin's films and his political past underwent radical reappraisal by critics and politicians alike. Restoration of his reputation began in Europe. In 1971, at the 25th Cannes Film Festival, Chaplin was given a special award for his body of work, and in the same year the French government made him a Commander of the Legion of Honor. A year later, he received a special Golden Lion Award for Career Achievement. More honors followed. In 1974 he received the Jussi Award (the Finnish equivalent of an Oscar) as Best Foreign Film-maker, for *Modern Times* and *The Great Dictator*; and in the same

year he was made an Honorary Life Member of the Directors' Guild of America. But the honor that must have given him the greatest pleasure and satisfaction came in 1·972.

After twenty years of exile, Chaplin was allowed back into the United States to receive a Special Academy Award at the 44th Oscars' ceremony, held in the Dorothy Chandler Pavilion, Los Angeles. Chaplin was introduced by the President of the Academy, Daniel Taradash, as the person "who made more people laugh than anyone in history". The Award was given "to Charlie Chaplin for the incalculable

effect he has had in making motion pictures the art form of this century." He presented Chaplin with his Oscar.

There followed a long standing ovation from a highly-enthusiastic audience. Chaplin was clearly overcome. He waited, tears in his eyes, until he felt he had to gently gesture them to be silent. He said very little, and ended by saying: "Words seem so futile, so feeble. Thank you for the honor of inviting me here, and oh, you're wonderful, sweet people."

Taradash then returned to Chaplin's side to add a bowler hat and a cane to the Oscar.

Previous pages
Left: The exile returns. Chaplin lands at
Kennedy Airport, New York City, en route
to Los Angeles to receive his Academy
Award, April 3, 1972.
Right top: Chaplin is the picture of
happiness as he reads press accolades on
the morning after he received his Academy
Award, April 11, 1972.
Right below: While in Los Angeles,
Chaplin made time to visit some of his old
Hollywood colleagues, among them Jackie
Coogan, Georgia Hale, and Martha Raye.
He also attended a party organised in his
honor by Walter Matthau, at the Pacific
Pallisades.

Opposite: An emotional Chaplin
acknowledges the applause of the star-
studded audience at the Dorothy Chandler
Pavilion, Los Angeles, after receiving his
Special Academy Award on April 10, 1972.
Above: Chaplin receives his Légion
d'Honneur Award on the opening night of
the Cannes Film Festival, May 15, 1971.

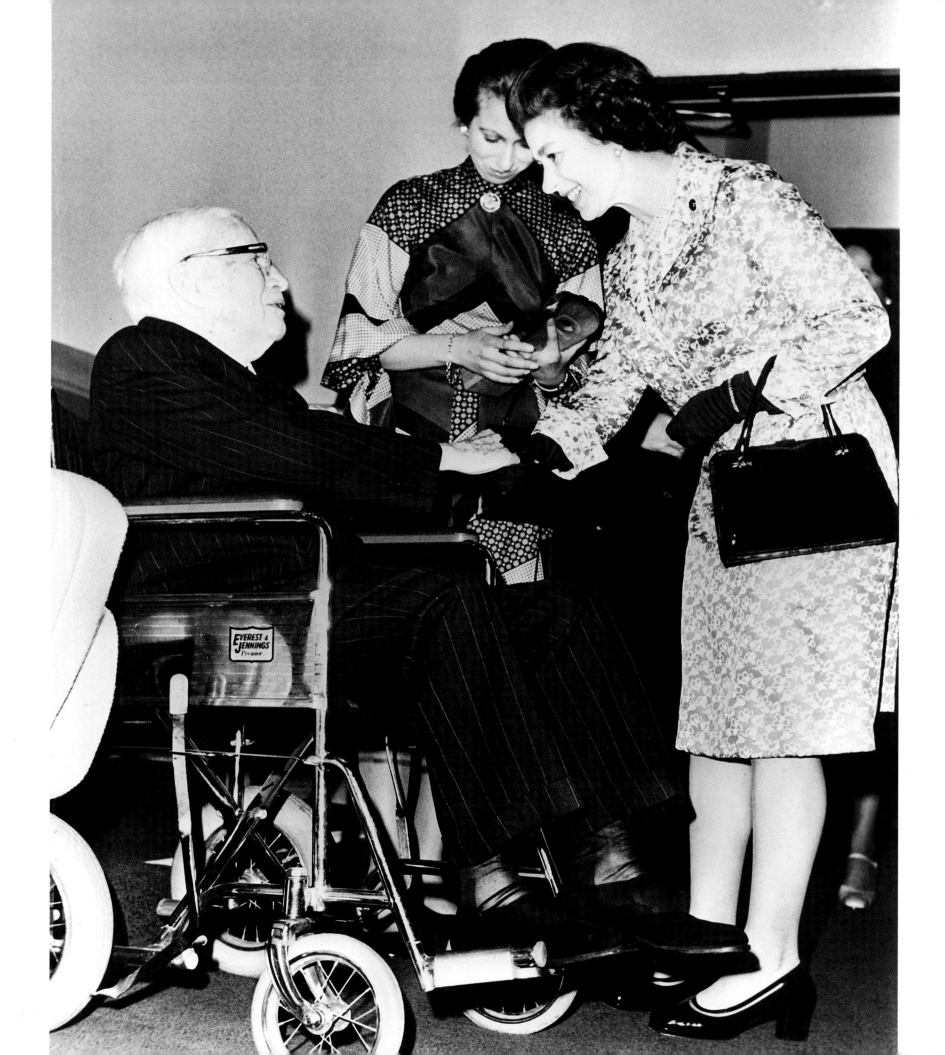

Reappraisal and Rewards

The shooting of *A Countess from Hong Kong* was completed on May 11, 1966, and the final edit contained the last shot of Chaplin on screen, as a ship's steward suffering from sea-sickness. The film premiered at the Carlton Cinema in London's Haymarket on January 5, 1967, and ten weeks later at the Sutton Theater, New York City. It was panned by critics in both the United States and the United Kingdom. Chaplin was typically aggressive in adversity. In what was now a ripe old age, he responded by saying: "If they don't like it, they're bloody idiots".

But the 1972 Academy Award brought about a total change of heart.

The world loved him, and he loved the world. His professional happiness was made complete with the presentation of another Oscar the following year. At the 45th Academy Awards, Chaplin received his first and only competitive Oscar. It was for Best Original Score, the music he wrote for the now twenty-year-old *Limelight*. The film was eligible as it had not previously played for two weeks in Los Angeles and so only qualified in 1972. Chaplin had always had a particularly soft spot for his own music. He used to hum his own film scores as he walked about the set.

Art-house cinemas around the world began to show Chaplin's feature films in what Chaplin himself described as his "renaissance". It was not all easy-sailing. There were other candidates for the role of Best Ever Movie Comedian – Buster Keaton, W. C. Fields, Harold Lloyd, and Laurel and Hardy among them. Strangely, the last country to hold out against the re-instatement and re-acknowledgement of Chaplin as *the* film genius was that of his birth. Not until after his death was Chaplin seen as a hero in Britain.

End Title

In July 2002, a quarter of a century after Chaplin's death, previously confidential papers of the British Foreign Office were released to the public. The papers revealed that successive British governments had strenuously opposed the notion of honoring the Little Tramp with a knighthood. There was criticism of Chaplin's acceptance of a prize awarded by the Communist-sponsored World Peace Council in June 1954, and condemnation of both his politics and morals which lasted into the early 1970s. Lord Cromer, British Ambassador to the United States, concluded that Bob Hope should be a preferred candidate for a knighthood.

The establishment succumbed to popular pressure. In May 1975, accompanied by Oona, Annette, and Christopher James, Chaplin went to Buckingham Palace. Now in a wheelchair, he entered the Investiture Hall, the band struck up the theme from *Limelight*, the Queen tapped him on each shoulder and placed the KBE insignia around his neck. She thanked him for what he had done, and said that his films had helped her a great deal. He was then wheeled to a position from which he watched the rest of the ceremony.

Above: After the knighthood, tea at The Savoy… The celebrants are (*left to right*) Nikki Sistovaris, Annette, Josephine, Chaplin, Oona, Christopher, Geraldine, and Jane, March 4, 1975.

Left: One of the last pictures taken of Chaplin. The occasion was the Wine Festival in Vevey, hence the glasses, and with Chaplin are Oona and his daughter Annette (*right*), August 10, 1977.

Goodbye Charlie

In 1976, Chaplin suffered a stroke and lost some of his powers of speech, an ironic tragedy for a man whose best work had never needed words. From then on, his health steadily deteriorated. According to Chaplin, in his youth a gypsy had prophesied that he would die at the age of eighty-eight. He reached that age in 1977, after an extraordinary life that had taken him from the slums of south London to everlasting fame. In making almost a hundred films, he had revolutionized both the content and style of screen comedy. He had hobnobbed with some of the most famous figures of the 20th century, and had outraged the most powerful nation on earth. Despite all this, Chaplin remained frightened that he would not be remembered.

He had hoped to make one last film, to be called *The Freak* – a strange and morbid fairy tale about Sarapha, a woman that sprouts wings and can fly. The part was written for his daughter, Victoria, whom Chaplin believed had great comic capabilities. Victoria wanted to do it; Oona didn't want it done, saying of Chaplin: "I can have him alive or have him die making the film". The day after she heard the film was not to be made, Victoria eloped with French actor Jean-Baptiste Thierrée.

Chaplin died in his sleep on Christmas Day, 1977, surrounded by his entire family, with the exception of Geraldine, who was filming in Spain – he would have appreciated her professionalism. He once described the Little Fellow as, "a tramp, a gentleman, a poet, a dreamer, a lonely fellow always hopeful of romance and adventure," words which might well serve as an epitaph for Chaplin himself.

Above: The funeral of Charlie Chaplin at the cemetery of Corsier-sur-Vevey, near Lake Geneva, Switzerland, on December 27, 1977. In a bizarre disinterment, the grave was robbed in March 1978 and the coffin later found in a cornfield. It now lies under six feet of concrete.

Above: Eighty children dressed as the Tramp gather near his statue in the Square Chaplin, Vevey, April 16, 1989. The statue was unveiled to celebrate the centenary of Chaplin's birth.

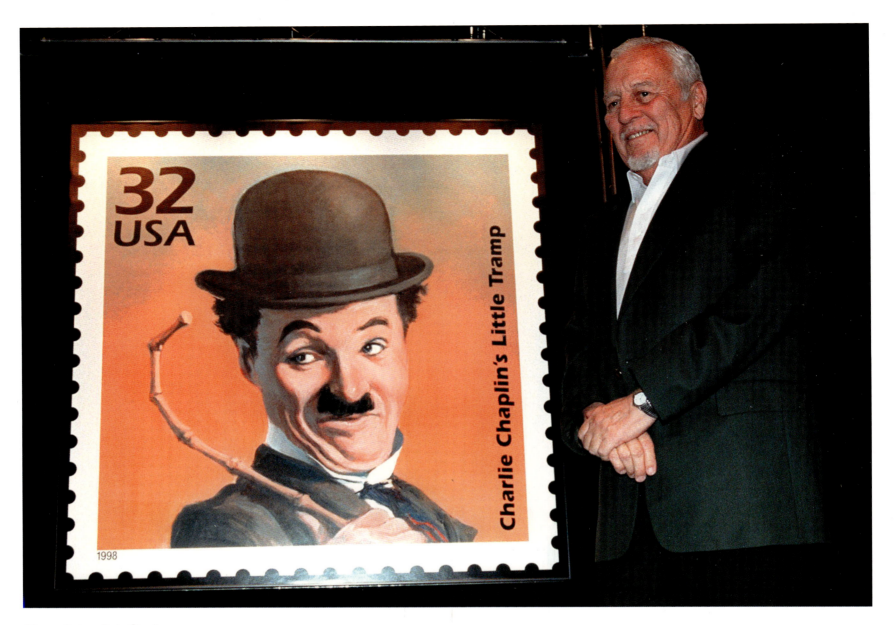

Above: Sydney Earle Chaplin stands beside a reproduction of the US postage stamp that features his father, January 1, 1998. The stamp was designed by caricaturist Al Hirschfeld and was one of a set of thirty honoring "the most memorable people" in each decade of the 20th century.

Above: The Great Dictator's moustache goes under the hammer at Christie's Film and Entertainment Auction, December 9, 2004. It was expected to reach a price of between £3,000 and £5,000, but sold for almost £18,000. The note reads: "To Maurice – thank you for your book – merci!", and is dated 1946. Maurice Bessy was later to co-author another book, *Monsieur Chaplin, ou le rire dans la nuit* (*Monsieur Chaplin, or the Laugh in the Night*), which was published in 1952.

Picture Credits

All images in this book are courtesy of Getty Images, we would also like to thank Jonathan Hyams at Michael Ochs Archive and Mitch Blank for their help. The following images have further attributions:

Agence France Presse: 37, 136, 145, 174

American Stock Archive: 59l

Apic: 12, 103

Chicago History Museum: 83

Imagno: 104, 112, 115

John Kobal Foundation: 65, 80l, 99, 100

Gene Lester: 90l

Michael Ochs Archive: 7, 11, 14, 90r

Popperfoto: frontispiece, 4, 8, 18, 20, 32, 35, 44, 45t, 52, 55, 63, 66, 69, 73, 97, 102, 129br, 131, 134, 137, 139b

RDA: 165

Horst Tappe: 147

Time & Life Pictures: 22, 24, 25, 27, 30, 31, 33, 40, 41, 42, 43tr, 43bl, 43br, 49, 51, 91tr, 95, 107, 122, 124, 128br, 129tr, 129bl, 153, 154, 155, 156b, 164, 173